Journey To The

MW00966038

This essay breaks through the misconc⟨
tional gender stereotypes and establishe⟨ ⟨ ⟨⟨⟨⟨ ⟨⟨⟨
framework for gender equity. At once personal and philosophical, the author's journey begins with a letter to God, asking, "Why
are you called HE?" Her struggle and inspiration will resonate
with anyone who has ever asked the same question.

*As I read ... Journey to the Father, I was immediately impressed with
the simplicity and clarity of style, together with the depth and profundity of insights it contained ... which in my opinion, should be shared
as widely as possible.*

William Hatcher, Ph.D.
Philosopher, Writer, Professor of Mathematics, retired
Author of *Love, Power, and Justice; Logic & Logos; Minimalism*

*... a thoughtful, beautifully written essay exploring the seeming
incongruity between the masculine founding face of the Bahá'í
Revelation, with its use of masculine terminology for God, and the
Faith's principle of equality and complementarity between the sexes.
The author provides welcome insights to our understanding of the profound issues raised. I look forward to her next essay focusing on "the
feminine" side of the equation. Highly recommended.*

Anne M. Pearson, Ph.D.
Adjunct Professor of Religious Studies, University of Waterloo

*Bravely presenting her findings as a truly personal "journey" driven
by a series of meditations and awakenings, Ms. Vanderwagen offers
knowledge unfettered by any doctrinaire or apologist point of view.
The reader comes away with a renewed understanding of the intricate
equipoise between the male and female principles. This is valuable.*

Richard M. Landau, M.A.
TV Producer and Host, CTS TV Faith and Interfaith Programming
Author of *What the World Needs to Know About Interfaith Dialogue.*

Journey to the Father

NEW PERSPECTIVES

ON GENDER AND

THE BAHÁ'Í REVELATION

JOELL ANN VANDERWAGEN

JOURNEY PUBLICATIONS
TORONTO

Care has been taken to trace ownership of copyright material contained in this text. The author will gladly receive any information that will enable her to rectify any reference or credit line in subsequent editions.

For information write: Journey Publications
P.O. Box 1363, Station K
Toronto, Ontario
Canada M4P 3J4

Or email: journey_publications@sympatico.ca

To order this book directly from the publisher, visit the website for price and shipping charges to your location.

Website Address: www3.sympatico.ca/journey_publications

National Library of Canada Cataloguing in Publication

Vanderwagen, Joell, 1946-
      Journey to the Father: new perspectives on gender and the Bahá'í Revelation / by Joell Vanderwagen

Includes bibliographical references.
ISBN 0-9684720-1-X

1. Equality—Religious aspects—Bahai Faith. 2. Sex roles—Religious aspects—Bahai faith. 3. Polarity. 4. Dualism. 5. Bahai women. 6. Bahai Faith. I. Title.

BP370.V352003   297.9'3'082   C2003-901737-0

Editing by Kathryn J. Dean
Design by Jodi Franklin/Julia Ames

Contents

Foreword

As I read through Joell Vanderwagen's essay, titled *Journey to the Father*, I was immediately impressed with the simplicity and clarity of style, together with the depth and profundity of the insights it contained. Coming from a North American background and having embraced the Bahá'í Faith as an adult, Ms. Vanderwagen encountered certain difficulties in reconciling the Bahá'í principle of gender equality with what she experienced as the "male face" of the history of the Bahá'í Revelation. Her meditations on this question led her to a number of insights which, in my opinion, should be shared as widely as possible. Among the points which Ms. Vanderwagen makes are the following:

- We know from the Bahá'í Writings that the human soul is not gendered. Thus, human spiritual identity of souls is primary (preexistent) and gender differentiation is physical and secondary.

- Gender differentiation is a lateral polarity of equals, not a hierarchical relation of dominance.

- Gender differentiation in all its forms fulfills a Divine purpose and serves rather than hinders the advancement of women, when properly understood.

- The dominance of strong male figures in Bahá'í history does not represent male power seeking but just the opposite: the willing self-sacrifice of male power and privilege in order to create a spiritually safe environment in which women are free to develop all of their potential.

- 'Abdu'l-Bahá, as the Perfect Exemplar of all Bahá'í virtues, provided a model for chaste but spiritually deep friendships between men and women.

This list is not exhaustive but it does serve to give the reader some idea of the quality of insight to be found in Ms. Vanderwagen's essay. At the end, she promises that there is more to come. Let us hope for and look forward to this consumation.

William Hatcher
Quebec City
April 2002

Preface

Dear Reader,

This small book has been eight years in the making and it is with gratitude that I finally commit it to print. The inspiration contained here seemed to have been given to me in trust to be shared with people everywhere who are struggling to understand what it means to be a woman or a man in today's world.

Because this is an essay recounting a spiritual adventure, I recommend that it be read straight through (without prior reference to the Notes marked by numbers), in order to share the sense of the experience and unfolding of its logic. As a preface to the story, I have provided a short introduction to the Bahá'í Faith on the next page.

The numbered Notes at the end provide a more detailed overview of the history, key historical figures, and Sacred Writings of the Bahá'í Faith. They were added at the recommendation of my editor so that readers from all backgrounds could better understand the context of the story and the meaning of various references.

I wish to thank Susan Lyons and members of the Literature Committee of the National Spiritual Assembly of the Bahá'ís of Canada for their painstaking reviews, helpful suggestions, and encouragement. I give special thanks to Dr. William Hatcher for his advice and rounds of inspiring consultation about the philosophical underpinnings of the topic. And finally, a heartfelt thank you goes to all friends and family who contributed, each in their own way, during the gestation period.

Joell Ann Vanderwagen

The Bahá'í Faith

Bahá'ís believe that God has given humanity a new Revelation for this day. Twin Prophets — Bahá'u'lláh and His Herald, the Báb — appeared in Persia (Iran) in the mid-nineteenth century, proclaiming the long-awaited Coming of Age of the human race. This Revelation, they said, ushered in a process of momentous change, involving the disintegration of old structures and institutions and the corresponding birth of a new global civilization.

Intrinsic to this consummate evolution, at once both spiritual and material, is the responsibility for independent investigation of truth and elimination of prejudice. The generating principles of this new age include:

- Recognition of the oneness of God — that all of the great religions spring from a common Source. They share eternal spiritual principles while differing in social teachings, revealed according to the needs of their time.

- Recognition of the oneness of humanity — that underlying our magnificent diversity is an essential unity.

- The equality of men and women.

- The harmony of science and religion.

- Elimination of extremes of wealth and poverty in an economic system based upon spiritual values.

- Universal education.

- Use of a universal auxiliary language.

- Establishment of a world federation of nations to bring global justice and peace.

Part 1

The Tree of Life

INTRODUCTION

The Revelation of Bahá'u'lláh establishes the equality of women and men as a fundamental verity of the new world order, stating that men and women alike reveal the attributes of God.[1]† In the Bahá'í Writings, we are told that one of the organizing principles of the universe is the principle of "pairing" (hence the division of humanity into two complementary genders)[2] and that the tension between these opposites is the source of motion and creativity in the universe. We are also told that neither the human soul nor its Creator, God the Unknowable Essence, is characterized by gender.[3]

Paradoxically, however, the Bahá'í Faith presents a male "face" to the world. God is described with metaphors such as *Father* and *King*; the Word of God is revealed through human males, called *Manifestations*; and the English translation of the Writings, following the conventions of seventeenth-century Oxford English, use entirely masculine nouns and pronouns to refer both to God and to people in general. The chain of infallible authority that guides the Bahá'í Community is passed from the Manifestations of God (The Báb and Bahá'u'lláh) to the Exemplar ('Abdu'l-Bahá) to the Guardian (Shoghi Effendi), and finally to the Universal House of Justice, where it will rest for at least a thousand years.

---

† The numbers refer to the Notes at the end of this book (beginning on page 37)

It is fair to say that this paradox — this seeming contradiction between the principle of equality of the sexes and the solely male founding language and authority figures of the Faith — is a source of discomfort to many Bahá'ís and is sometimes perceived as a significant obstacle by newcomers investigating the Faith.

The purpose of this essay is to share some new, and positive, perspectives on the concepts of gender in the Bahá'í Revelation, resulting from the author's personal investigation and experience. This investigation was not pursued in the form of academic research, but unfolded as a dialectic between the Writings and personal inspiration, which illumined some of the mystical realities and inherent logic of the founding process of the Faith.

THE WRITER'S CULTURAL CONTEXT

In the Western world, the first wave of the women's movement in the mid-nineteenth century was about practical matters such as legal and political rights and access to education and employment. The second wave, in the mid-twentieth century, expanded the focus to include the more subtle issues of gender bias in language, history, and theology. Women endeavoured to bring to light their own stories and perspectives and gathered the courage to question traditional male authority figures in fields such as medicine, politics, and organized religion.

For the first time, on a wide scale, the very nature of patriarchal religion was openly questioned and often rejected. A corresponding search was begun for more "feminine" expressions of the Divine, both within the traditional structures and outside them. Re-examination of the original texts of the Bible revealed a much broader range of feminine imagery and language than had been conveyed in the old English translations. New translations of the Bible also adopted a variety of conventions for inclusive language: some as basic as using words like *person* or *humanity* when referring to both men and women; others as radical as calling God either "Father" or "Mother" or both, with terms like "God, the Father-Mother almighty" (Cooper, *Our Father in Heaven: Christian Faith and Inclusive Language for God,* pp. 21–40).

The search by Westerners outside their traditional organized religions included exploration of Native spirituality, with its respect for Mother Earth; research into ancient goddess religions; development of new theories of Creation spirituality; and the practice of disciplines such as yoga, meditation, and psychotherapy. This collective endeavour has been called the "feminization" of religion — characterized by awareness of the sacred and interconnected nature of all Creation and by a turning inward for inspiration grounded in one's own intuition and experience (Lenz and Myerhoff, *The Feminization of America: How Women's Values Are Changing Our Public and Private Lives,* pp. 138–56).

THE WRITER'S EXPERIENCE

Coming of age in North America in the 1960s and 1970s — at the time of the peace, civil rights, environmental, and feminist movements — I participated in this feminist spiritual search and found it deeply rewarding. During these explorations, however, I also discovered the Bahá'í Revelation. The authenticity of the

3

Principles and the compelling spirit of the Bahá'í Writings struck a deep cord. But as a modern North American woman, what was I to make of its patriarchal qualities, which seemed at one fell swoop to reverse all the progress of the sixties and seventies?

While I was investigating the Faith, over a period of about four years, this question initially loomed large. However, over time, the need to build a personal relationship with the God who spoke to me in the Writings and to be part of His spiritual community gradually superseded the gender issues, and in June of 1995, I declared my belief in Bahá'u'lláh and joined the Bahá'í Community. For several weeks thereafter, I experienced a great sense of elation and heightened spiritual awareness.

PAIN AND ANGER

Abruptly, however, the "gender issue" crashed back into my consciousness, this time with the feeling of being run over by a truck. The prayers were the most painful part of the experience. In my most intimate relationship with God, I was supposed to call myself *he* and in turn be addressed as *son*. I was supposed to identify myself with a larger group called *men* and *mankind*. Thus, the words that connected me to love simultaneously told me that I did not exist.

Suddenly, God, the source of all life and love, felt hostile and alien. HIS presence was represented by a set of stern male figures who seemed to both ignore me and yet demand full control over my life. Although there were formal pronouncements about equality in the Writings, it seemed as if God never spoke *through* women or directly *to* women — only *about* women as if they were a separate species.

"Why can't you speak to *me?*" I asked. "Is there something intrinsically wrong with *her, she,* and *woman* that you can't use these words in the text?" "If I'm to call you 'Father,' why can't you at least call me 'daughter'?" I felt the crushing pain of rejection.

All the Holy Days commemorate the heroic acts of solely male founding figures. Men in the community can identify with these powerful archetypal figures and events, and in surrendering themselves, feel reborn in their image. But where is our story told? Don't women need role models too? Is there nothing heroic or sacred about women's experiences? Don't they need to see God acting through a woman? Don't they need to see HER face? I felt the crushing pain of total invisibility.

Until this point I had been able to dismiss sexist concepts in older traditions as reflective of their times and to view the male authorities as products of those power structures. Progressive people assumed that our culture had evolved in the intervening several thousand years, and they were making serious efforts to adapt ancient texts and traditions to modern consciousness.

Now, it seemed we'd gone straight back to the past. The language and stories shouted that women were only guests at a male activity. Oh, yes, we were "equal," but first we had to pass through a glass wall and become honourary males. In return for the protection of the Covenant and the benefits of inclusion in this worldwide community, we had to give up our identity.

I felt I had to maintain some distance from all this, preserving the connection to my inner voice, female identity, and self-respect. The idea of "surrendering" seemed like an act of psychic suicide: rather than being reborn or transformed, I would merely disappear.

A belief in the maleness of God and the infallibility of designated male authority figures also seemed to present dangers for power relationships between men and women. The unconscious logic would be: God is male; therefore maleness is godlike. The effect would be to strengthen men's egos and diminish women's confidence and self-respect. It would reinforce old Western classical notions that spirit is male, matter is female; spirit is good, matter is evil; reason is male, instinct is female; and it would imply that women should accede to male authority regardless of their own experience of the truth.

I also became aware that my pain was amplified by my personal history. My grandmother's father had died when she was three. My mother's father had died when she was eight. I had never known my father because my parents had divorced soon after I was born and gone their separate ways. After becoming an adult, I began to realize there was a void inside me where "father's love" should have been. It was odd enough to pray to "Our Father Who Art in Heaven" as Jesus taught when I had no concept of father, but it was made worse by the fact that Bahá'u'lláh did not address me as "daughter." How could I feel loved if He didn't talk to me? I felt the burden of three generations of pain weighing down on me.

Cut off from my Creator, I thrashed about in the "dark night of the soul." When a week had passed and the pain hadn't lifted, my feelings increased to the level of desperation. I wondered what to do.

Then I recalled that this is a God who says He wants to have a personal relationship with us. I remembered that a good relationship requires communication and sometimes struggle, that the opposite of love is not anger — it's indifference. Thus, I had a choice. I could either walk away from the relationship or I could engage in it. To engage in it meant to confront God with my pain and anger, taking seriously the principle of an independent investigation of truth.

A LETTER TO GOD

So I sat down with pen and paper and began to write to HIM.
This outpouring took the form of a two-page letter to God, in
July 1995, which included the following questions:

> Why are you called HE?
>
> Why are all the Manifestations male?
>
> Why are women so invisible in the Writings?
>
> Am I wrong to ask these things?
>
> I feel that I cannot teach the Faith until I am at peace
> with these questions. Please guide me on the right path.

Having finished the letter, I put it aside and hoped to get on with
my life. Little did I anticipate a swift response.

THE RESPONSE

The next morning, I went out for groceries and stopped to talk
with one of the shopkeepers, an old acquaintance who was a
devout Christian. On this morning she told me, with great enthu-
siasm, about a new minister she had discovered. However, as she
described his ideas, an undercurrent of prejudice and fanaticism
began to reveal itself. It soon became evident that the man was
actually a cultish leader preaching hatred toward anything that
fell within his hodgepodge definition of evil people, practices,
and religions. To make a long story short, I attempted to engage
in a discussion but gave up when I saw her eyes take on a
"demonic" glint that made me shudder. It seemed my friend had
crossed over the line from faith to fanaticism, reminding me of

the news stories of the day about militia and white-supremacist movements in North America.

I left the store shaken, feeling that I had been given a direct and vivid perception of the reality of the forces of fanaticism at large in the world — the same kind of forces that had surrounded the Báb. I suddenly felt grateful to be grounded in the Bahá'í teachings about unity and protected by the power of the Covenant. At a subliminal level, I perceived that when confronted with these fiendish energies, the male face of the Faith somehow seemed appropriate, focusing attention on the main issue: the new Revelation embodied in Bahá'u'lláh and His authority over those forces.

I struggled with how to respond to this experience — to never see her again or to somehow try to reach out to her. I concluded that as individuals we have a responsibility to respond to evil when it confronts us. Otherwise, each person, such as my friend, will become a link in a chain of fanaticism that can take over a society. I sat down for an entire day and composed a letter to her straight from my heart, speaking within her frame of reference as a Christian. I urged her to maintain her own powers of discernment to judge whether that man's ideas conformed to the teachings of Jesus Christ. That evening, I slipped the letter under the door of her shop.

The next day, a box of raspberries appeared on my porch with a note from her, thanking me for the inspiring letter and apologizing for her behaviour! Funny thing, only two days earlier I had been paralyzed with pain and anger and "unable to teach the Faith."

THE BÁB (The Gate, 1819–1850)[4]

Later in the day, I went for a walk, still filled with the awareness of these hateful forces, manifesting themselves in war, terrorism, and chaos throughout the world. I was reminded of the situation in Iran in the early days of the Bahá'í Faith, when the Báb first proclaimed the electrifying message of the new Revelation. Out of nowhere, a foreign thought planted itself in my mind:

> To be invisible is a protection. This is not a tea party, it is a war.
>
> There is a spiritual war unfolding for control of the planet.
>
> The martyrdom of the Báb was the first battle.
>
> The nature and ferocity of these forces were revealed at that time.
>
> The defence of the community is the responsibility of men.
>
> The Báb attracted the bullets to himself.
>
> The House of Justice is on the front lines in the creation of the new world order.
>
> The essence of being a Manifestation is sacrifice and servitude to bring order and peace to the world.

These ideas were accompanied by a wave of feeling and recognition: The Báb suddenly seemed very real. I felt a tangible sense of his suffering and courage in the midst of ferocious violence and hatred. He acted out an archetypal male role — that of the Warrior — offering up his body, attracting the bullets to himself, and preparing the way for Bahá'u'lláh.

It seemed clear that the essence of being a Manifestation of God was that of sacrifice and servitude. These figures do not represent worldly notions of male power. That is our fallible, human misinterpretation. If I mentally substituted the image of a woman in the Báb's role, it did not feel right. It seemed that God would not use a woman's body for a role involving public torture and martyrdom. This was a battle between men.

Later, I had these afterthoughts: Consider female birds whose colourings make them difficult to see and think of why many males have brilliant plumage — to distract attention away from the nest. During the persecutions of the 1980s in contemporary Iran, 90 percent of the Bahá'ís tortured and executed were male. I realized with astonishment that my questions had been answered on a primal level.

However, that was only the beginning. Every morning for the next two weeks I awoke to a river of images and ideas flowing through my mind, elaborating on the understanding of gender found in the Bahá'í Revelation. The concepts unfurled, like the petals of a flower, one day at a time. Then, over several years, these primary concepts expanded through additional inspiration, as well as through more systematic and logical development on my part.

BAHÁ'U'LLÁH (The Glory of God, 1817–1892)[5]

In my mind, when I awoke the next morning, I was with Bahá'u'lláh, chained deep within the blackness of the Síyáh-<u>Ch</u>ál dungeon, where He was confined by the forces seeking to exterminate the new Faith. While lying there in pain and confinement, a new Revelation of God appeared. The fragrances of heaven filled the chamber of torture. I am reminded of the experience of childbirth: in the midst of pain and confinement, a miracle is born. Supplanted by the glory of this miracle, the ego surrenders, desiring only to serve this new life with passionate love. At that time, I was not aware that, when Shoghi Effendi wrote the chapter describing this event in *God Passes By*, he gave it the following title: "The Birth of the Bahá'í Revelation."

Thus, through Bahá'u'lláh, God participated in archetypally female acts of heroism — courage in the face of possible torture and death in childbearing; selfless love and service to family and community; and development of inner peace and wisdom in the midst of outer social imprisonment. Both Bahá'u'lláh and His son, 'Abdu'l-Bahá, endured lives of confinement, just like Middle Eastern women of their day.

Yá Bahá'u'l-Abhá (Mirror image: O Glory of Glories)
Copyright © 1990 by S. Monjazeb

'ABDU'L-BAHÁ (Servant of the Glory, 1844–1921)[6]

On the second morning, I understood how the Revelation had turned the old world on its head. While 'Abdu'l-Bahá was voicing supreme frustration at His own imprisonment, Martha Root — designated by 'Abdu'l-Bahá as "the herald of the Kingdom" — was free to travel the world four times over. The first to respond to His *Tablets of the Divine Plan* (received by North American Bahá'ís in 1919), she covered the earth with the Word of God and helped establish the network of relationships that grew into the worldwide Bahá'í community.

In His role as Exemplar of the Faith, 'Abdu'l-Bahá represents the new human being who has a balance of masculine and feminine qualities and who can relate to and work with the opposite sex in a spirit of loving partnership. While only one generation earlier, Táhirih[7] (an early Bahá'í heroine) had addressed men from behind a veil, now 'Abdu'l-Bahá had personal relationships with early women believers and pioneers. He corresponded with them, met with them, was a guest in their homes, and travelled alone in their company.

As God calls the human race into its adulthood, the exterior veils and restrictions between the sexes can be removed as interior discipline develops within the individual. Having reconciled within himself the forces of reason and instinct, 'Abdu'l-Bahá exemplifies a central principle from which will come the generative energy of the new world order: friendship between men and women.

SHOGHI EFFENDI (Guardian of the Bahá'í Faith, 1897–1957)[8]

The third morning brought a vivid sense of the life of Shoghi Effendi. Designated as Guardian of the Faith, Commander-in-Chief, Architect, and Builder, Shoghi Effendi was charged with the task of building up the Bahá'í Administrative Order and its central institutions. I came to understand that the creation of large organizations was a quintessentially masculine activity. Beginning in tribal days, males organized themselves as groups, with a leader, in order to accomplish more than they could as individuals — whether in hunting or war or in building large structures. This involved behaving as one body whose actions were coordinated by the head.

As society evolved, the structures, activities, and organizations became more complex (the military, the church, the nation-state, the modern corporation). The Bahá'í Administrative Order, spanning the globe and encompassing the entire human race, will mark the apex and completion of that process of organizing human society. Shoghi Effendi equated the evolution of this gargantuan task with a military operation in which Bahá'u'lláh's "army of light" engaged the forces of darkness holding the globe in captivity.

As Commander-in-Chief, Shoghi Effendi exercised authority, set goals, devised strategies, and deployed "troops." While acting at the centre of a military operation was, again, a quintessentially masculine role, for him it was also a form of self-sacrifice and imprisonment, while the early pioneers (the majority of whom were women) went out to "conquer" the globe. [9]

14

THE UNIVERSAL HOUSE OF JUSTICE[10]

'Abdu'l-Bahá has said:

> The House of Justice ... according to the explicit text of the
> Law of God, is confined to men; this for a wisdom of
> the Lord God's which ere long will be made manifest as
> clearly as the sun at high noon.
>
> — 'Abdu'l-Bahá, Selections from the Writings, pp. 79–80.

"How will the answer be made manifest?" I asked. "Will it
be handed down from on high?" During those early days, when
the petals of the flower were unfolding in my mind, I found
myself reading The Hidden Words of Bahá'u'lláh.

> The best beloved of all things in My sight is Justice;
> turn not away therefrom if thou desirest me, and neglect it
> not that I may confide in thee. By its aid <u>thou shalt see with
> thine own eyes</u> and not through the eyes of others, and shalt
> know thine own knowledge and not through the knowledge of
> thy neighbour.
> [underlining added]
>
> — Bahá'u'lláh, Arabic Hidden Words, no. 2.

It seems that if we sincerely seek justice, we will be
rewarded with an understanding of what it is. In this case the
answer came to me that justice is not always served by treating
everyone in the same way. Hence Bahá'u'lláh turns our eyes to
the most important factors for achieving justice for women over
the long term:

1. Bahá'í laws mandating gender equality in the family.

2. Bahá'í laws giving priority to the education of women.

Family life provides a crucible for development of new attitudes and behaviour patterns in each generation, whose members will, in turn, bring those changes to all levels of society. Bahá'í laws specify the equality of wife and husband and require that decisions be made through the process of consultation. These laws are a radical departure from the practices of authoritarian decree and physical intimidation so common in the past (and present).

Universal education for women (with girls given priority over boys where resources are scarce) will provide women with the capacity to speak and act for themselves, as well as improving their effectiveness as mothers.

The House of Justice is not an end in itself but rather a means to an end. Its responsibility is to ensure that these laws are obeyed on a worldwide basis, in societies with vastly different cultures and at different stages of development. The practical implementation of these laws will ensure that equality of status and opportunity between men and women develops on a solid foundation from the grass roots up.

Thus, I felt assured that the composition of The House of Justice was appropriate for the state of the world at this time and for the tasks to be accomplished.

> Verily justice is My gift to thee
> and the sign of My loving-kindness.
> Set it then before thine eyes.

— Bahá'u'lláh, *Arabic Hidden Words*, no. 2.

THE TREE OF LIFE

In the Bahá'í Writings, the men of the Holy Family are referred to as *Branches* and the women as *Leaves*. In his letters, Bahá'u'lláh often addressed women with phrases such as "O My Handmaiden, O My Leaf." My first reaction was to be stung by the comparison. After all, branches must be more important than leaves because they are strong, permanent structures.

However, in one of my morning "awakenings" I gazed into the wondrous realities of nature and understood that the leaf is where the life process and creativity of the tree are located. The leaves conduct photosynthesis, turning the energy of the sun into food for the tree and ultimately the fruit. The branches create a structure to support the leaves and supply them with minerals and moisture.

A tree consists of branches and leaves; without either there would be no tree. Men and women can survive separately but they don't flourish. Whether single or married, they thrive in a community of friendship between men and women, in the context of chastity. When men and women act in harmony, the creativity of the universe flows through them.

Men are meant to be protectors[†] who create a space of peace and order in which the feminine qualities of society can

---

[†] Since the concept of men as "protectors" did not sound "politically correct" to modern ears, I was tempted to leave the idea out of this section. However, because it was clearly part of the original inspiration, I have decided to retain it while raising questions as to its

emerge.†† The examples of the founding figures of the Faith provide a healing, transformative vision for men.†††

On another level, the Administrative Order can be seen as the branches of the tree and individual Bahá'ís as the leaves. The institutional structure is the channel for disseminating the Revelation of Bahá'u'lláh and provides the framework for releasing the creative power of individuals.

---

meaning. 'Abdu'l-Bahá has stated that "man has dominated over woman by reason of his more forceful and aggressive qualities of both body and mind" (qtd. in *Star of the West*, p. 4). Perhaps, then, men are responsible for exercising a restraining or policing function with respect to male aggression. According to 'Abdu'l-Bahá:

> There are certain matters, the participation in which is not worthy of women. For example, at the time when the community is taking up vigorous defensive measures against the attack of foes, the women are exempt from military engagements ... It is the duty of men to organize and execute such defensive measures and not the women — because their hearts are tender and they cannot endure the sight of the horror of carnage, even if it is for the sake of defence. From such and similar undertakings the women are exempt.
>
> — *Paris Talks*, no. 59.6.

†† Perhaps the meaning of the phrase "a space of peace and order in which the feminine qualities of society can emerge" can be explained by analogy with the function of the *masculine* and *feminine* qualities within each individual. In this analogy, the masculine side functions as the guardian, evaluating the safety of the physical

My morning awakenings continued to be flooded with impressions of the beauty and richness of gender polarities. These meanings grew more complex, contrasting two ways of thinking about pairs of opposites. A new perspective within the Bahá'í Revelation struggled to emerge — one that could bring peace to the "war" between the sexes — a peace embracing positive, creative tension between equals.

---

and emotional environment and marshalling the individual's powers of assertion or defence. If the environment is perceived as safe, then the individual can let down his or her guard and enter into relationships of trust, cooperation, and nurturing.

††† Collectively, men can think of themselves as either protectors or destroyers of the life of the planet, the community, and the family. The *Utne Reader* devoted its entire May/June 1991 issue to the topic of "The New Politics of Masculinity." One section focuses on restoring the ancient concept of *husbandry*, saying:

> The essence of husbandry is a sense of masculine oblig-
> ation – generating and maintaining stable relationship
> to one's immediate family and to the earth itself. At its
> heart, husbandry reflects a bonding of both family and
> nature through a clear appreciation of the responsibility
> inherent in the role of provider, caretaker, and steward.
> ... A renaissance of husbandry will help heal the deep
> spiritual wound men now suffer. To actively practice hus-
> bandry, without domination or exploitation, can reawaken
> the male spirit from alienation and isolation.

Part 2

Equations without Dualism

COMPLEMENTARITY OF OPPOSITES

The Bahá'í Revelation states that the realm of Creation is based on the pairing of equal and complementary opposites. In a given pair, both halves are "good" and exercise the same amount of creative force in relation to one another — like two wings,[11] which power the flight of a bird, or two poles of a magnet, which have equal power of attraction and repulsion. Thus, strength and gentleness, reason and intuition, performance and contemplation, justice and mercy, initiative and response, masculinity and femininity are all positive attributes that should be balanced within the individual and society. The relationship between two complementary opposites can be called a *polarity* and can be visualized on a horizontal scale, as shown opposite (upper diagram).

According to the Writings, evil and good are not opposites. Rather, evil is the *absence* of good, just as darkness is the absence of light. Weakness is the absence of strength, not its opposite. The relationship between existence and non-existence can be called a *duality* and can be visualized on a vertical scale, as shown opposite (lower diagram).

The Writings teach that each created thing reveals an attribute of God and that all of these attributes are manifested in the human being, both male and female. Women and men are meant to develop all of the positive qualities and apply them appropriately. The absence of a quality, where it is needed, is a negative trait, whether in a man or a woman.

It would seem that the notion of complementarity means that each gender has the capacity to develop some of the positive qualities to a greater extent. For example, both men and women can be strong, but the male body has the capacity to develop physical strength to a greater degree. Correspondingly, the female body has the capacity to manifest grace and gentleness to a greater degree. The differences in this case are not deficiencies but a dynamic balance between two opposites.

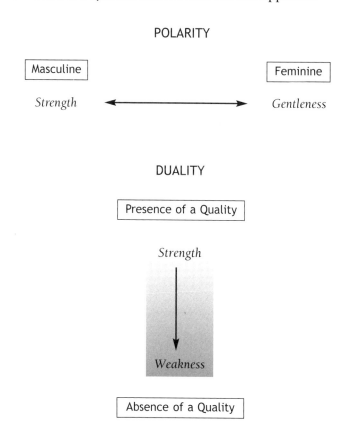

POLARITY

| Masculine | | Feminine |

Strength ←————————→ *Gentleness*

DUALITY

Presence of a Quality

Strength

Weakness

Absence of a Quality

21

DUALISM

The Bahá'í model seems to be a significant departure from ancient Hellenistic philosophies and cults that have influenced Western thought for over two thousand years. According to these beliefs, good and evil constitute a duality, and so, by analogy, do spirit and matter, male and female. According to Plato, the rational intellect was the path to the realm of the spirit (associated with the male) and the physical body was the source of evil, tying one down to rebirth in the fallen realm of matter (associated with the female).

In the creation of a child, according to Aristotle, the father's semen contained the *active* principle — the "form" of the child — which instructed the development of the *passive* matter supplied by the body of the mother. Divine creation of the physical world was explained according to this same analogy (Pantel, *A History of Women in the West*, pp. 46-81). Science can now tell us, of course, that both the father and the mother equally contribute their chromosomes to the DNA molecule, which directs the development of the child. One does not "instruct" while the other remains passive.

Aristotle also described the human being as one species, whose form was male. The female represented imperfection in the reproductive process, resulting in a deficiency of masculine qualities. Thus, the masculine represented perfection and the feminine imperfection (Pantel, pp. 46–81).

These "old world order" stereotypes, based on the notions of classical dualism, are still very much with us today.

For example, when a boy is developing his male identity and fails to exhibit sufficient "masculine" qualities, he is often defined as "feminine" (following Aristotle's line of thought). The worst criticism is to be called "a girl." Paradoxically, according to this mindset, if he should give help or protection to those who are in need of it, he would at the same time implicitly be denigrating them as "weak." As a corollary, of course, he cannot ever allow himself to admit need or vulnerability.

A persistent assumption that needs reconsideration is the still common tendency to describe the feminine principle as passive in relation to the active masculine principle. Passivity is the quality of inert objects that act according to the laws of nature and have no will of their own — a brick placed in a wall, for instance, or a leaf floating down a river. In human terms, this is exemplified in the hierarchical relationship between master and slave, where there is no exercise of will or reciprocity on the part of the slave.

Many cultures have held such thinking up as a model for the relationship between men and women, but this does not mean the stereotype is true. The human soul has been endowed with consciousness and the capacity to exercise free will, regardless of the gender of the body. Passivity has negative connotations. It belongs on a vertical scale, as part of a duality — as the *absence* of activity or conscious will.

ACTIVE AND RECEPTIVE PRINCIPLES

What, then, would be the equal and complementary opposite of the active principle? If to act is to take initiative, then the opposite is to be receptive, to respond. A good example of this is the relationship between *speaking* and *listening*. A speaker who finds himself alone in front of rows of empty chairs will not likely bother to talk to the chairs because they are passive and inert objects. A human audience, on the other hand, is engaged and receptive, taking in new ideas and formulating inner responses.

People engaged in a dialogue take their turns as listener and speaker. A receptive listener encourages the speaker to clarify and fully express her thoughts and then thinks about what she has said. The listener then responds and speaks according to his own experience and perspective. This is the basis for thorough consultation, which, according to the Writings, will yield new insights into the truth of a matter and bring solutions to a problem. The Writings about consultation tell us that the receptive principle of listening is at least as important as, if not more important than, the active principle of speaking. In this context of true equality and complementarity, it is valid to think of receptivity as residing in the feminine part of the masculine-feminine polarity. [†]

[†] It may be noted that some contemporary authors use the term *passive* in a positive way. According to this interpretation, passivity can mean acceptance of things which we are powerless to change; surrender to the will of God; the conscious choice to let things unfold in their own way; or the decision to wait, lie low, and remain dormant for a time.

However, in such cases, the outer passivity is accompanied by an inner human response or decision. It would seem that lack of awareness and inner response could be equated with spiritual death. The ambiguity surrounding the term *passivity* indicates the need for further discussion of its implications for gender stereotyping.

MASCULINE AND FEMININE: A DIAGRAM

Similar pairs of qualities can be described in many ways — such as initiative and response, doing and being, performance and contemplation — all of which need to be expressed in a balanced way in the lives of individuals and society. The following diagram provides a visual framework for locating different pairs of qualities in relation to one another, as either *polarities* (equal and complementary opposites) or *dualities* (existence vs. non-existence of qualities).

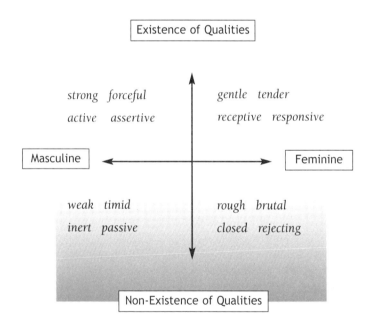

Such an exercise can inspire ongoing discussions as we develop greater insight into the meaning of positive spiritual qualities or virtues and negative gender stereotypes. For example, men are sometimes stereotyped as rough and brutal. However, according to the diagram above, roughness and brutality would not be masculine qualities, but rather, the absence of appropriate feminine qualities.[††]

[††] *Clarifying Gender Terminology.* There are at least three sets of common terms used to describe gender differences:

- *male* and *female*
- *men* and *women*
- *masculine* and *feminine*

Writing this essay involved a struggle to find clear and precise language which could capture the subtleties of the topic. Below, I offer the definitions that evolved out of my analysis. Awareness of the distinctions among these three sets of terms can help us build a language of gender that incorporates new perspectives and attitudes.

Male and *Female* are biological terms used to describe different body types and physical functions found in nature. On the animal level, these functions are largely unconscious and governed by instinct.

Men and *Women* are adult human beings. Like animals, they have physical bodies with unconscious functions and instincts. In addition, they have conscious awareness and powers of reason and intuition associated with their spiritual nature. According to Bahá'í teachings, their souls are beyond gender.

The concepts set out in the preceding pages emerged during my initial period of inspiration. However, I was still searching for a more explicit explanation of why we call God "Father" and I undertook a more conscious review of the Sacred Writings. On the following pages I share some of my insights based upon logical inferences from specific Bahá'í teachings, as well as some of my personal struggles with how to relate to a spiritual Father.

Masculine and *Feminine* are descriptive terms for qualities traditionally associated with males and females, within a cultural context. The observation that different body types and biological roles fostered the development of different traits necessary to fulfill those roles led, in turn, to the training of male children to be "masculine" and female children to be "feminine," often to the exclusion of the opposite traits. On a positive level, this training ensured that each gender would be responsible for exercising certain positive qualities for the benefit of family and society.

Unfortunately, this approach sometimes restricted individuals to one-dimensional sets of human qualities. Even worse, negative stereotypes evolved. Roughness and brutality became associated with masculinity, when these traits actually represented uncontrolled animal instincts and the absence of feminine qualities of care and gentleness. Seductiveness and passivity became associated with femininity, when they were actually inappropriate expressions of animal instincts and the absence of active and assertive masculine qualities.

It is the premise of this essay that the terms *masculine* and *feminine* connote a range of positive human qualities — indeed, spiritual virtues — that are requisite for the complete development of human beings of both genders.

IN THE GLORY OF THE FATHER

The Bahá'í Writings teach that the entire human race, in its cultural development over time, progresses through the same stages as a child does in its growth through infancy, childhood, adolescence, and adulthood. The Writings also tell us that this period of history is the turning point, when humanity is to progress from adolescence into adulthood. Logically, it would seem that these teachings can help explain why the Writings refer to God as "He" and "Father."

We know that a baby is closest to its mother during infancy and early childhood. It would be logical, then, that during humanity's earliest phases of development, the Divine would have been experienced as Mother. Indeed, archaeological evidence reveals the widespread existence of goddess religions in early times. Existing cultures of Indigenous peoples preserve living examples of a cosmology in which Mother Earth is a spiritual link to the Creator.

It is commonly understood that when the child — particularly the boy — reaches a certain stage, he needs to separate from his mother and identify with his father, who traditionally initiates him into the larger society and his masculine role. Correspondingly, it seems logical that when the human race reached the end of its "childhood," God the Unknowable Essence appeared in masculine form, at the beginning of the Adamic Cycle,[12] to lead humanity through the next stages of its development.

God, who is beyond our comprehension, also has an

intimate personal relationship with us. God describes this relationship in terms relating to our own experiences — hence, the analogies of *lover and beloved* or *parent and child*. But, at this time in history, "Father" is meant to be the predominant metaphor for God's relationship with us.

HAVING A SPIRITUAL FATHER

While this explanation made sense to me as a logical extrapolation of the Bahá'í teachings, I still struggled to understand what it meant on a personal level. How should I experience a Spiritual Father? I consciously tried to relax my fear of old stereotypes and to meditate about what it would mean to have a perfect father. These thoughts came to me:

> God created my physical body and eternal soul.
>
> He loves me.
>
> I can trust that He will assist me.
>
> He is my guide and my refuge, the help in peril.
>
> Through His prophets, He teaches me the spiritual laws.
>
> These laws are a safe pathway, a light in the darkness, a firm rudder on the ship of life.
>
> Wherever I go — in whatever circumstances I find myself — I can always take hold of His outstretched hand.

This inspiration told me that the Father's love energizes a woman's masculine side and honours and cherishes her feminine side. The Father gives her the courage, strength, and purpose to make her way in the world. Thus protected, she is free to express feminine radiance and tender warmth for those around her. Thus guarded, she can allow herself to trust and reach out to love.

In renewing the Eternal Faith of God, the Bahá'í Writings are filled with messages of unconditional love, healing, and mercy that can be associated with a nurturing mother. However, the metaphor of "Father" would seem to convey additional messages that are necessary for our passage from adolescence to adulthood. This is related to the God who disciplines and challenges us, who informs us that we are accountable for our choices and teaches us the meaning of justice through reward and punishment. If we think of "organization" as a masculine principle, it makes sense that this Revelation has provided humanity with a Divine plan for the institutions of a global society.

GROWING UP

Given that humanity is in its adolescence and given that public power, at the highest levels, is almost entirely held by dominant males, it would be fair to say that the world is run by adolescent males who are in need of a strong father to help them grow up. Thus, Bahá'u'lláh has come to us *in the glory of the Father.*[13]

For humans, fatherhood is a matter of conscious choice. While the mother is always involved when a baby is born, the father can be a thousand miles away or even unaware of the conception. Thus, the role of the father is a social construct and boys need role models and guidance appropriate for their time and place. The Revelation provides a strong father archetype that can be activated in every man.

However, as humanity enters its adulthood, individuals are released from the rigid gender stereotypes of the past.[14] The roles of mother and father will always be grounded in certain physical realities, calling for the development of corresponding skills and qualities, but beyond that, individuals are called upon to develop both their masculine and their feminine sides. In this wholeness, our humanity will come into full bloom.

CONCLUSIONS

The concepts described in this essay were part of the initial outpourings in response to the questions in the letter that I wrote to God: Why are you called HE? Why are all the Manifestations male? Why are women so invisible in the Writings?

This experience has been illuminating, not only in terms of the new perspectives that unfolded, but also in terms of lessons I learned about the process itself. It seems that if we are honest with ourselves and honest with God about our concerns and if we seriously attempt to investigate the truth, we will be rewarded with great bounties of wisdom.

THE OTHER HALF OF THE EQUATION

While this essay deals with issues concerning the male "face" of the Faith and the founding process, it doesn't elaborate on the feminine side of the equation. This will be the subject of other writings still in development.

Afterword

One last part of the story needs to be included with this essay. When I gave the above text to Dr. William Hatcher (author of *The Law of Love Enshrined; Love, Power, and Justice;* and many other works familiar to Bahá'ís), I also asked his opinion about the interpretation of the following Tablet of Bahá'u'lláh:

> That which hath been in existence had existed before, but not in the form thou seest today. The world of existence came into being through the heat generated from the interaction between <u>the active force and that which is its recipient.</u> These two are the same, yet they are different. Thus doth the Great Announcement inform thee about this glorious structure.
>
> Such as communicate the generating influence and such as receive its impact <u>are indeed created through the irresistible Word of God</u> which is the Cause of the entire creation, while all else besides His Word are but the creatures and the effects there of. Verily thy Lord is the Expounder, the All-Wise. [underlining added]
>
> — Bahá'u'lláh, "Lawh-i-Hikmat" in *Tablets of Bahá'u'lláh*, p. 140.

I specifically asked him how the concept of complementary opposites (polarities) might compare with the concept of *the active force and that which is its recipient.* My concern had been evoked by statements made by Bahá'í scholars who equated the *active* force with God and the *receptive* quality with humanity, characterizing humanity as passive/feminine. <u>The Tablet does not appear to equate God with the active force</u>, but says that <u>both are created by God</u> and that *these two are the same, yet they are different.*

Dr. Hatcher called the next day and said that he had been inspired with the following insight, quoted as follows:

Imagine a sphere viewed from the side, divided into the left hemisphere and right hemisphere by a vertical slice down the middle. The sphere represents:

BEING AND THE SOUL

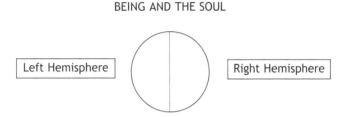

Next, imagine a horizontal line going from left to right, with a node at each end. These nodes represent the magnetic poles, one positive and the other negative. The poles create a continual flow of energy between them, which is the electromagnetic field. The internal flow of energy is created by an internal dialogue between these polarities.

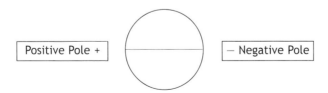

In the individual, the left hemisphere represents LEFT BRAIN polarities such as "reason" and "analysis." The right hemisphere represents RIGHT BRAIN polarities such as "intuition" and "synthesis." The inner dialogue between these two generates the flow: we analyze, then we synthesize. We have an inspiration, then we evaluate it.

INTERNAL DIALOGUE

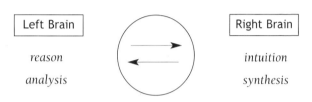

Left Brain		Right Brain
reason		*intuition*
analysis		*synthesis*

In reference to 'Abdu'l-Bahá's analogy of the bird, the configuration of the "bird with two wings" represents BEING, whereas the flight of the bird represents BECOMING. The dialogue between the left and right wings creates the capacity for becoming. This inner dialogue engenders the capacity for pro-active interaction — self-initiated actions. At the same time, it engenders a receptivity which reflects itself in the capacity for reaction. The *internal* dialogue generates *inner* development/autonomy.

External progress is generated by dialogue *between two beings.* The dialogue has to be initiated by one of the beings. The possibility for true dialogue depends upon exercise of the inner polarities within each being which in turn generates the capacity for pro-action and receptivity. Each being is capable of initiating, responding to, and maintaining a dialogue.

EXTERNAL BECOMING

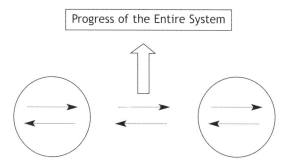

Progress of the Entire System

This process is called consultation, and it generates the progress (the forward movement) of the entire system, much as a two-bladed propeller, rotating on a fixed plane, generates the forward movement of an entire aircraft. The process would not work if there were only one blade.

In closing, I should mention that Dr. Hatcher's interpretation of the quotation about *the active force and that which is its recipient* inspired some debate among reviewers of this book, who, in turn, offered their own interpretations. I hope this discussion will continue.

The Bahá'í approach to interpretation of the Sacred Writings is governed by the instructions of the founders. On His passing, Bahá'u'lláh designated His son, 'Abdu'l-Bahá as the sole interpreter of His Writings. 'Abdu'l-Bahá, on His passing, conferred that role on Shoghi Effendi, the Guardian of the Bahá'í Faith.

In turn, Shoghi Effendi provided the following guidance for individuals in a letter written on his behalf on November 17, 1933:

> A clear distinction is made in our Faith between authoritative interpretation and the interpretation or understanding that each individual arrives at for himself from his study of its teachings. While the former is confined to the Guardian, the latter, according to the guidance given by the Guardian himself, should by no means be suppressed. In fact such individual interpretation is considered the fruit of man's rational power and conducive to better understanding of the teachings, provided that no disputes or arguments arise among the friends and the individual himself understands and makes it clear that his views are merely his own.

— *Lights of Guidance*, no. 88.

1. GENDER EQUALITY

Know thou … that … women are accounted the same as men, and God hath created all humankind in His own image, and after His own likeness. That is, men and women alike are the revealers of His names and attributes, and from the spiritual viewpoint there is no difference between them.

— 'Abdu'l-Bahá, *Selections*, no. 38, pp.79–80.

Women and men have been and will always be equal in the sight of God. The Dawning-Place of the Light of God sheddeth its radiance upon all with the same effulgence. Verily God created women for men, and men for women. The most beloved of people before God are the most steadfast and those who have surpassed others in their love for God, exalted be His glory.

The friends of God must be adorned with the ornament of justice, equity, kindness and love. As they do not allow themselves to be the object of cruelty and transgression, in like manner they should not allow such tyranny to visit the handmaidens of God. He, verily, speaketh the truth and commandeth that which benefitteth His servants and handmaidens. He is the Protector of all in this world and the next.

— Bahá'u'lláh, qtd. in *Women*, p. 26.

Divine Justice demands that the rights of both sexes should be equally respected since neither is superior to the other in the eyes of Heaven. Dignity before God depends, not on sex, but on purity and luminosity of heart. Human virtues belong equally to all!

— 'Abdu'l-Bahá, *Paris Talks*, no. 50.10.

2. PRINCIPLE OF PAIRING

> *From the pairing of even the smallest particles in the world of being are the grace and bounty of God made manifest; and the higher the degree, the more momentous is the union.* "*Glory be to Him Who hath created all the pairs, of such things as earth produceth, and out of men themselves, and of things beyond their ken*"[Qur'an 36:36, and cf. 51:49]. *And above all other unions is that between human beings, especially when it cometh to pass in the love of God. Thus is the primal oneness made to appear; thus is laid the foundation of love in the spirit.*

—'Abdu'l-Bahá, *Selections*, no. 87, p. 119.

3. GENDER AND THE HUMAN SOUL

> *Know thou that the distinction between male and female is an exigency of the physical world and hath no connection with the spirit; for the spirit and the world of the spirit are sanctified above such exigencies, and wholly beyond the reach of such changes as befall the physical body in the contingent world.*

— 'Abdu'l-Bahá, qtd. in *Women*, rev. ed., 1990, no.10.

4. THE BÁB

Known as the Báb (The Gate), Siyyid 'Alí-Muḥammad was born in 1819 in the Persian city of S͟híráz. He is the first of the two Prophet-Founders of the Bahá'í Faith. In 1844, the Báb proclaimed Himself to be the Promised One of Islam, the Qá'im, and said that His mission was to prepare the way for the imminent coming of "Him Whom God shall make manifest." His followers, known as Bábís, carried His teachings across the land, electrifying the population, who were oppressed by ignorance and despotism.

Becoming alarmed, the Shí 'ih Muslim clergy rejected His claims, and the government imprisoned the Báb in the fortresses of Máh-Kú and then Chihríq. The Báb's followers were subjected to brutal persecution and massacres. On July 9, 1850, in the city of Tabríz, the Báb was placed before a firing squad in the barracks square, bound up with a devoted follower, and hung from a rope. The event is described by Nabíl in *The Dawn-Breakers: Nabíl's Narrative of the Early Days of the Bahá'í Revelation.*

As soon as they were fastened, a regiment of soldiers ranged itself in three files, each of two hundred and fifty men ... The smoke of the firing of the seven hundred and fifty rifles was such as to turn the light of the noonday sun into darkness. There had crowded onto the roof of the barracks, as well as the tops of the adjoining houses, about ten thousand people, all of whom were witnesses to that sad and moving scene.

As soon as the smoke had cleared away, an astounded multitude were looking upon a scene which their eyes could scarcely believe. There, standing before them alive and unhurt, was the companion of the Báb, whilst He Himself had vanished uninjured from their sight. ... They set out in a frenzied search for Him and found Him, eventually, seated in the same room which He had occupied the night before, engaged in completing His interrupted conversation, with Siyyid Ḥusayn [His amanuensis/secretary]. An expression of unruffled calm was upon His face. ... "I have finished My conversation ... ," the Báb told the [official]. "Now you may proceed to fulfil your intention."

Sám Khán [the Colonel of the regiment which had attempted the execution] was ... stunned by the force of this tremendous revelation. He ordered his men to leave the barracks immediately, and refused ever again to associate himself and his regiment with any act that involved the least injury to the Báb.

No sooner had Sám <u>Kh</u>án departed than
[Colonel] Áqá Ján <u>Kh</u>án-i-<u>Kh</u>amsih ... volunteered to
carry out the order for execution. On the same wall and
in the same manner, the Báb and His companion were
again suspended, while the regiment formed in line to
open fire upon them. ... This time their bodies were
shattered and were blended into one mass of mingled
flesh and bone, ... The very moment the shots were
fired, a gale of exceptional severity arose and swept over
the whole city. A whirlwind of dust of incredible density
obscured the light of the sun and blinded the eyes of the
people. The entire city remained enveloped in that darkness from noon till night (pp. 512–15).

Some of the followers of the Báb managed to hide His
body in various places of concealment and protect it until, in
1909, the wooden casket was finally entombed on Mount
Carmel, at the site that would become the Shrine of the Báb, the
centrepiece of the Bahá'í World Centre in the city of Haifa in the
Holy Land.

5. BAHÁ'U'LLÁH AND THE MAID OF HEAVEN

Known as Bahá'u'lláh (the Glory of God), Mírzá Ḥusayn-'Alí was
born in 1817 to a noble family of Núr in Mázindarán, Persia (now
Iran). Without formal education, He was recognized even as a
child for his astonishing wisdom and immense compassion. In
1844, at the age of twenty-seven, He became a follower of the
Báb and emerged as a leader of the Bábí movement. In 1852,
two years after the Báb's execution, when the Bábís were subjected to intense persecution, He was put in chains for four
months in an underground prison known as the Síyáh-<u>Ch</u>ál in
Ṭihrán. It was here that the Revelation of God first appeared to
Him. In his book *God Passes By*, Shoghi Effendi describes these
events:

Such a Revelation was ... born amidst the darkness of a subterranean dungeon in Ṭihrán — an abominable pit that had once served as a reservoir of water for one of the public baths of the city. Wrapped in its stygian gloom, breathing its fetid air, numbed by its humid and icy atmosphere, His feet in stocks, His neck weighed down by a mighty chain, surrounded by criminals and miscreants of the worst order, oppressed by the consciousness of the terrible blot that had stained the fair name of His beloved Faith, painfully aware of the dire distress that had overtaken its champions, and of the grave dangers that faced the remnant of its followers — at so critical an hour and under such appalling circumstances the "Most Great Spirit" ... descended upon, and revealed itself, personated by a "*Maiden*", to the agonized soul of Bahá'u'lláh. ...

In His Súratu'l-Haykal [also spelled Súriy-i-Haykal] (the Súrih of the Temple) He thus describes those breathless moments when the Maiden, symbolizing the "*Most Great Spirit*" proclaimed His mission to the entire creation: "*While engulfed in tribulations I heard a most wondrous, a most sweet voice, calling above My head. Turning My face, I beheld a Maiden — the embodiment of the remembrance of the name of My Lord — suspended in the air before Me. So rejoiced was she in her very soul that her countenance shone with the ornament of the good-pleasure of God, and her cheeks glowed with the brightness of the All-Merciful. Betwixt earth and heaven she was raising a call which captivated the hearts and minds of men. She was imparting to both My inward and outer being tidings which rejoiced My soul, and the souls of God's honoured servants. Pointing with her finger unto My head, she addressed all who are in heaven and all who are on earth, saying: 'By God! This is the Best-Beloved of the worlds, and yet ye comprehend not. This is the Beauty of God amongst you, and the power of His sovereignty within you, could ye but understand. This is the Mystery of God and His Treasure, the Cause of God and His glory unto all who are in the kingdoms of Revelation and of creation, if ye be of them that perceive.'*"

In His Epistle to Násiri'd-Dín S̲h̲áh [entitled Lawḥ-i-Sultán], His royal adversary, revealed at the height of the proclamation of His Message, occur these passages which shed further light on the Divine origin of His mission: *"O King! I was but a man like others, asleep upon My couch, when lo, the breezes of the All-Glorious were wafted over me, and taught Me the knowledge of all that hath been. This thing is not from Me, but from One Who is Almighty and All-Knowing. And He bade Me lift up My voice between earth and heaven, and for this there befell Me what hath caused the tears of every man of understanding to flow. … His all-compelling summons hath reached Me, and caused Me to speak His praise amidst all people"* (pp. 100–102).

After freeing Him from prison, the government banished Him to Bag̲h̲dád in Iraq, where he lived for ten years with His family and a growing body of followers. Then the Persian government persuaded the Ottoman government to banish Him further, to Constantinople (now the city of Istanbul). On the eve of his departure in 1863, Bahá'u'lláh gathered his closest followers in the Garden of Riḍván (Garden of Paradise) and told them that He was the Promised One of All Ages foretold by the Báb.

After several months in Constantinople, he was again banished to Adrianople (now the city of Edirne) at the western end of the Turkish Empire. There, he publicly proclaimed His Mission and wrote proclamations to the kings and rulers of the earth, calling on them to establish world peace, justice, and unity. Finally, in 1868, Turkish authorities banished Bahá'u'lláh, along with His family and some of His followers, to the horrible prison city of 'Akká, located in the Holy Land.

There, in the strictest confinement, they suffered from disease and hardship. In spite of this, he continued His proclamations to the rulers of the earth and set out the foundation principles of the new Revelation of God for this day, contained in numerous books and some 15,000 Tablets. In 1877 He was allowed to move outside the prison city to the Mansion of Bahjí. He spent his final years there and ascended in 1892.

6. 'ABDU'L-BAHÁ

In His Will, the "Book of My Covenant," Bahá'u'lláh appointed His eldest son, 'Abdu'l-Bahá, as his successor and the authorized Interpreter of His Writings. Originally named 'Abbás, His son chose the name 'Abdu'l-Bahá (Servant of The Glory) after His father's passing. His Father also referred to 'Abdu'l-Bahá as "The Master" and "The Mystery of God."

'Abdu'l-Bahá was born on May 23, 1844, the very night of the Declaration of the Báb, and He lived until 1921. Throughout His life, He served His Father and shared in His exiles and imprisonments until He was set free after the Young Turk Revolution in 1908. In 1911 He began His historic journeys to Europe and North America to proclaim His Father's message. His speeches to the North American Bahá'ís and the general public are recorded in the book *The Promulgation of Universal Peace*.

Although Bahá'ís do not regard 'Abdu'l-Bahá as a Prophet in His own right, they honour His unique station by capitalizing pronouns referring to Him, and they believe that He was a stainless mirror reflecting Bahá'u'lláh's light and teachings.

7. TÁHIRIH

Fátimih Umm Salamih, who came to be known as Táhirih, was born the same year as Bahá'u'lláh in the city of Qazvín in northern Persia. From childhood, she was a prodigy of renowned intelligence and beauty. Her father, who was a *mujtahid* (the highest rank of divine in Shí'ih Islam), had her educated in Qur'ánic scholarship, and she went on to become a theologian and poet, widely esteemed for her brilliance and novel views. Because she was not a man, however, she could not play a formal clerical role, and conversed with men only from behind a screen or veil.

She associated with a group of scholars who anticipated the coming of a prophet and a time of spiritual rebirth. Although she never met Him face to face, the Báb appeared to her in a dream and, through correspondence, she became one of His first eighteen followers.

> Through her eloquent pleadings, her fearless denunciations, her dissertations, poems and translations, her commentaries and correspondence, she persisted in firing the imagination and in enlisting the allegiance of Arabs and Persians alike to the new Revelation, in condemning the perversity of her generation, and in advocating a revolutionary transformation in the habits and manners of her people.

— Shoghi Effendi, *God Passes By,* p. 73.

While the Báb was imprisoned in the fortress of Chihríq, eighty-one of His followers gathered for a conference in the hamlet of Badasht, a gathering organized by Bahá'u'lláh. Each of the followers received new names, and Fáṭimih (also known as Qurratu'l-'Ayn) became Ṭáhirih. When some of her more rigid and conservative fellow disciples later complained to the Báb about her disregard for tradition, the Báb replied, "What am I to say regarding her whom the tongue of Power and Glory has named Ṭáhirih [the Pure One]?" (Nabíl, *The Dawn-Breakers,* p. 293).

As events unfolded, it became clear to many participants that the underlying meaning of the conference was to concretize the break with the past represented by the new Revelation. It was Ṭáhirih, the lone woman, who enacted this dramatic purpose, according to the following account quoted by Nabíl:

> "Suddenly the figure of Ṭáhirih, adorned and unveiled, appeared before the eyes of the assembled companions. Consternation immediately seized the entire gathering. ...To behold her face unveiled was to them inconceivable. Even to gaze upon her shadow was a thing which they deemed improper, inasmuch as they regarded her as the very incarnation of Fátimih [the daughter of Muhammad] ... ."

> — Shaykh Abú-Turáb, qtd. in *The Dawn-Breakers*, pp. 294–95.

According to another source, she exclaimed,

> "'I am the blast of the trumpet, I am the call of the bugle,' i.e. 'Like Gabriel, I would awaken sleeping souls.'"

> — T.K. Cheyne, qtd. in *The Dawn-Breakers*, pp. 297–98, ftn. 2.

Then, according to the first account,

> "Quietly, silently, and with the utmost dignity, Ṭáhirih stepped forward. ... .A feeling of joy and triumph had now illumined her face. She rose from her seat and, undeterred by the tumult that she had raised in the hearts of her companions, began to address the remnant of that assembly. Without the least premeditation, and in language which bore a striking resemblance to that of the Qur'án, she delivered her appeal with matchless eloquence and profound fervour. ...

> "Immediately after, she declared: 'I am the Word which the Qá'im is to utter, the Word which shall put to flight the chiefs and nobles of the earth!' ...Ṭáhirih invited

45

those who were present to celebrate befittingly this great occasion. 'This day is the day of festivity and universal rejoicing,' she added, 'the day on which the fetters of the past are burst asunder. Let those who have shared in this great achievement arise and embrace each other.'"

"The object of that memorable gathering had been attained. The clarion-call of the new Order had been sounded. The obsolete conventions which had fettered the consciences of men were boldly challenged and fearlessly swept away. The way was clear for the proclamation of the laws and precepts that were destined to usher in the new Dispensation."

—*The Dawn-Breakers*, pp. 295–97.

The gathering dispersed and Ṭáhirih made her way to Ṭihrán. There, she reached the pinnacle of her fame. Regarded with enormous respect and affection, she taught the principles of the New Dispensation to the women of the capital who flocked to her presence. However, the noose of opposition was tightening and, one night, in August 1852, she was arrested and taken to a garden outside the city. There, she was strangled with her own white scarf, a martyr to the New Faith. Her fame spread across Persia and onward to the capitals of Western Europe, where many were captivated by her story (Shoghi Effendi, *God Passes By*, pp. 75–76).

8. SHOGHI EFFENDI, BAHÍYYIH <u>KH</u>ÁNUM, RÚ<u>H</u>ÍYYIH <u>KH</u>ÁNUM

In His Will and Testament, 'Abdu'l-Bahá appointed His eldest grandson, Shoghi Effendi, to be His successor, and conferred upon him the title Guardian of the Cause of God. Shoghi Effendi was born in 1897 in 'Akká — the same prison city in which

Bahá'u'lláh and the Holy Family had lived in exile — and grew up with his extended family in the home of 'Abdu'l-Bahá. He was educated at the American University in Beirut and then at Oxford University in England. The word *Effendi* means "sir" or "mister" and is added as a term of respect. When he went away to school, 'Abdu'l-Bahá "gave him the surname of Rabbání, ... and this was also used by his brothers and sisters. In those days there were no surnames, people were called after their city, their eldest son or a prominent person in their family" (Rabbání, *The Priceless Pearl*, pp. 4, 17).

In going to Oxford, Shoghi Effendi prepared himself to become the official translator of the Bahá'í Writings. For this task he used the seventeenth-century English of the King James Bible because it most closely matched the exalted forms of Persian and Arabic used by Bahá'u'lláh. While at Oxford, he was notified of 'Abdu'l-Bahá's death in 1921 and given the instructions for the role he was to play, contained in the Will and Testament. However, being too overcome with grief to assume these unexpected and onerous responsibilities, Shoghi Effendi asked his great-aunt, Bahíyyih Khánum, The Greatest Holy Leaf, daughter of Bahá'u'lláh, to act as the head of the Faith and to manage its affairs in his absence. After about a year, he returned to take up his office (Momen, *A Basic Bahá'í Dictionary*, pp. 208–9).

The central mission of his life was to establish the practical institutions of the Faith — the worldwide Administrative Order set out in the Writings of Bahá'u'lláh and 'Abdu'l-Bahá. He maintained communication by mail and telegraph with the far-flung followers and instructed them in the creation of Local

Spiritual Assemblies and, eventually, the creation of National Spiritual Assemblies. He acquired land and planned the layout of the Bahá'í World Centre on Mount Carmel in Haifa, Israel, and promoted the completion of the first Bahá'í Temple in Chicago, as well as others around the world. He created an authoritative history of the founding of the Bahá'í Faith with his translation of *The Dawn-Breakers: Nabíl's Narrrative of the Early Days of the Bahá'í Revelation* and his authorship of *God Passes By*. His instructions, his interpretation of the Writings, and his commentaries on current events in light of God's unfolding plan are collected in a series of books, including *The Advent of Divine Justice* and *The Promised Day Is Come*.

Throughout the first arduous eleven years of Shoghi Effendi's role as the Guardian, his closest companion and sustainer was The Greatest Holy Leaf — who had lived through the hardships, exiles, and imprisonments of her Father, Bahá'u'lláh. When she died in 1932, he was devastated with grief and asked the Bahá'í world to observe nine months of mourning in her honour. Among the many messages he penned to the Bahá'ís are the following words:

> How can my lonely pen, so utterly inadequate to glorify so exalted a station, so impotent to portray the experiences of so sublime a life, so disqualified to recount the blessings she showered upon me since my earliest childhood — how can such a pen repay the great debt of gratitude and love that I owe her whom I regarded as my chief sustainer, my most affectionate comforter, the joy and inspiration of my life? My grief is too immense, my remorse too profound, to be able to give full vent at this moment to the feelings that surge within me.

Only future generations and pens abler than mine can, and will, pay a worthy tribute to the towering grandeur of her spiritual life, to the unique part she played throughout the tumultuous stages of Bahá'í history, to the expressions of unqualified praise that have streamed from the pen of both Bahá'u'lláh and 'Abdu'l-Bahá, the Centre of His Covenant, though unrecorded, and in the main unsuspected by the mass of her passionate admirers in East and West, the share she has had in influencing the course of some of the chief events in the annals of the Faith, the sufferings she bore, the sacrifices she made, the rare gifts of unfailing sympathy she so strikingly displayed — these, and many others stand so inextricably interwoven with the fabric of the Cause itself that no future historian of the Faith of Bahá'u'lláh can afford to ignore or minimize.

— *Bahíyyih Khánum: The Greatest Holy Leaf*, pp. 31-32.

In 1937 Shoghi Effendi married a Westerner, Mary Maxwell, of Montreal. She took the name Rúhíyyih Rabbání and was referred to as Rúhíyyih Khánum (*Khánum* means "lady" or "madam"). Their partnership symbolized the union of East and West in the Bahá'í Faith and she became his secretary and his representative at international conferences. Later, Shoghi Effendi appointed her as a *Hand of the Cause of God*.

In her book about his life, entitled *The Priceless Pearl*, she provides not only a summary of the progress of the Bahá'í Community under his leadership but also an intimate glimpse of Shoghi Effendi's spiritual radiance and his trials and sufferings. She provides samples of the statistics that Shoghi Effendi compiled, noting that in 1921, he listed 35 countries opened to the Faith and that by 1957, he was able to list 254 — with Bahá'ís residing in about 4,500 centres. By 1957, one thousand Local Spiritual Assemblies had been formed (Rabbání, pp. 391-93).

Shoghi Effendi passed away unexpectedly in 1957, during a trip to London, England. In the midst of her grief, Rúḥíyyih Khánum notified the Hands of the Cause and other Bahá'ís. From all over the world, they converged on London for his burial. The Hands of the Cause (individuals appointed by the Guardian and charged with specific duties of protecting and propagating the Faith) acted as Chief Stewards, directing the affairs of the Faith until the Universal House of Justice was elected in 1963. Amatu'l-Bahá Rúḥíyyih Khánum went on to travel the world as a teacher, a spokesperson, and often, an appointed representative of the House of Justice, until her death at the end of the millennium, in the year 2000. She was the last of the Holy Family.

9. MARTHA ROOT

Born in 1872 in Cambridge Springs, Pennsylvania, Martha Root had an inquisitive and adventurous spirit. She studied Latin, Greek, French, German, and English Literature at Oberlin College and the University of Chicago and went on to become a newspaper editor, an unusual career for a woman at that time. In 1902 she became a foreign correspondent and sent back vivid descriptions of her travels in Europe. The following account of her life and work is based upon her biography by M.R. Garis, *Martha Root: Lioness at the Threshold.*

The year 1908 proved to be a turning point, when she met Roy Wilhelm and Thornton Chase, two early American Bahá'ís who had journeyed to the Holy Land and met with 'Abdu'l-Bahá in the prison city of 'Akká. She was intrigued by their stories and embarked on an intense period of research.

"Martha was struck with the simplicity and grandeur of the Bahá'í teachings. The events were historically provable, her logical mind latched on to their practicality, and her spirit was touched by the beauty and divine essence of the writings" (Garis, p. 45).

The following year, she became a Bahá'í and plunged into the activities of the growing network of American Bahá'ís — organizing conferences, speaking, and writing. Her extensive article about the Bahá'í principles appeared in the *Pittsburgh Post* in September 1909, and in what was to become a pattern, she obtained several hundred copies and sent them to people all over the world (Garis, p. 48).

When 'Abdu'l-Bahá was released from prison and made His historic journey to America in 1912, she was twice able to meet with Him personally. However, during the course of the Great War, between 1914 and 1918, communication with the Holy Land was cut off. Then, in 1919, at the National Convention in New York City, the American Bahá'ís were able to hear the contents of the *Tablets of the Divine Plan*, which 'Abdu'l-Bahá had addressed to them. Martha Root was the first to respond to 'Abdu'l-Bahá's detailed instructions to the American Bahá'ís to take the message of the Revelation to the rest of the world. Her first journey was by ship to cities of South America — down the east coast with stops in Brazil, Uruguay, and Argentina. Then overland to Chile, and up the west coast to Peru, Panama, and finally, Cuba.

Although she knew no one, she would meet people who could put her in contact with important officials, key organizations, and newspapers, and translate for her. She would provide articles for the newspapers and books for the local libraries, give several speeches a day, and then move on to the next city. She collected the names and addresses of her new friends and continued to correspond with them and send them material about the Faith. This meant that she sent out hundreds and hundreds of letters and thousands and thousands of books and pamphlets. In addition, her newspaper articles were reprinted in numerous other papers, which were copied and distributed by the new Bahá'ís in each country.

The physical hardships and dangers of travel were also daunting: storms at sea, bitter cold or suffocating heat, riots and political turmoil, epidemics of deadly diseases, and the daily grind of finding safe food and lodging as a woman alone. In order to get from Argentina to Chile and continue up the west coast, she first had to cross the Andes on mule back in the middle of winter! This is an excerpt from her description of that journey:

> The trip by mule back over the "top of the world," for the Andes are among the highest ranges, ... was thrilling enough for the most sensational. To pray the Greatest Name among these minarets of God was to glimpse the glory of the Eternal ... .The ancient trail led 10,400 ft. above sea level.The people on mule back were infinitesimal specks clinging to mighty terraces ... ants ... huddled on the edge of jagged peaks, frozen chasms, and stiffened mountain torrents. ... A detour through one dark tunnel took over an hour in stumbling, slipping blackness in which the frightened mules shied and fell.

> — Root, "*A Bahá'í Pilgrimage*," qtd. in Garis, p. 104.

Martha kept 'Abdu'l-Bahá informed with regular and detailed accounts of her travels. He responded with immense joy and, in one of His letters to her, said the following:

> It is clear and evident that the power of the Kingdom is aiding thee ... and the power of the Holy Spirit is supporting thee. ... In brief, thou art really a herald of the Kingdom, a harbinger of the Covenant. ... Thou art now planting a tree that shall everlastingly put forth leaves, blossoms and fruit and whose shadow shall grow in magnitude day by day.

> — 'Abdu'l-Bahá, qtd. in *"Pilgrimage,"* qtd. in Garis, pp. 111–12.

Martha returned home to care for her ailing father, until he died in 1922. Then, at age fifty, she left Pennsylvania to become a citizen of the world. She travelled through the United States, and in March 1923 set sail from Seattle to Yokohama, Japan. From there she went to China, Hong Kong, Australia, and New Zealand. She also undertook a long voyage to Durban, South Africa, and from there, she travelled up the coast of Africa to the Red Sea.

At last, on March 8, 1925, she landed in the Holy Land — the fulfilment of her heart's desire: to meet Bahíyyih Khánum, and to confer with Shoghi Effendi, now the Guardian of the Bahá'í Faith. The significance of her stay cannot be summarized in a few short words, so readers are referred to the account in her biography, *Martha Root: Lioness at the Threshold.* From Bahíyyih Khánum she heard stories of the history of the Faith and descriptions of 'Abdu'l-Bahá's work to help the people of Palestine which, had led to his being knighted at the end of the war (Garis, pp. 207–18).

Shoghi Effendi asked her to be his emissary to Geneva, Switzerland, to help establish an International Bahá'í Bureau, thus beginning her European travels. After a fruitful time in Geneva, where she participated in several international conferences, Martha proceeded to Germany, Austria, Holland, and several Balkan countries. Over the next four years, she criss-crossed Europe, visiting Hungary, Serbia, Romania (where she had her first meeting with Queen Marie, who embraced the teachings), Bulgaria, Czechoslovakia, England, Spain, Lithuania, Latvia, Estonia, Finland, Sweden, Norway, Belgium, Greece, Turkey, and Egypt. November 1929 found her back in the Holy Land, to bask in love and spiritual renewal.

From there, she undertook a dangerous journey through Syria, Iraq, and Iran, during which she visited Bahá'ís all over Iran and made pilgrimages to sites important in the lives of the Báb, Bahá'u' alláh, 'Abdu'l-Bahá, and Ṭáhirih. Shoghi Effendi had given her a letter of introduction to the Bahá'ís, in which he announced the visit of

> the Leader of the men and women teachers, Her holiness Miss Martha Root. ... It is incumbent and obligatory upon all the beloved of God and handmaidens of the Merciful One in that sacred land to receive that noble soul with their hearts and souls ... . For this unique believer with an astonishing power and matchless courage and constancy has raised the cry of Ya Baha'u'-alláh [sic] in the loftiest places ...

— Shoghi Effendi to Root, qtd. in Garis, p. 338.

The Spiritual Assembly of Tehran sent a letter to America, describing the effect of the arrival in Persia of our beloved spiritual sister Miss Martha Root. ... People who, as proved by history, looked upon foreigners with enmity and bitterness, and considered association with them as contrary to religion, now, thanks to Bahá'u'- alláh's Teachings, shed tears of joy at the sight of their American sister. ... [We] perceived ... the profound effect which Miss Martha Root's words ... produced upon those hearing her, who could scarcely repress the flow of tears of exultation, and who rejoiced in the realization of true love and oneness taught by Bahá'u' alláh.

— Holley, qtd. in Garis, p. 352.

From there, Martha travelled through India, Burma, China, and Japan, finally arriving back in America in January 1931. In 1932 she returned to Europe for five and a half years. In 1936 she came back to America and then, at age sixty-five, went on to her fourth visit to Japan and then China. Her stay in Shanghai was cut short by the outbreak of war. Caught in the middle of a bombing attack, she managed to escape on a ship bound for the Philippines. However, they landed in Manila only to be struck by a major earthquake and typhoon!

Undaunted, Martha proceeded to India, where she spent over fifteen months traversing the country. According to her biography, "A fair-sized book could be written on Martha's incredible teaching trip through India. Her travels were vast, her lectures and meetings seemingly beyond human scope ... The gargantuan spirit in the fragile frame was eloquently received" (Garis, p. 452).

At the end of 1938, she set off for Australia, from there intending to return home. However, she made it only as far as Honolulu, where she died on August 10, 1939 — felled by the cancer she had been fighting off and on since 1912, the pain of which sometimes slowed but never stopped her travels.

10. THE ADMINISTRATIVE ORDER

The Bahá'í Revelation is unique in the history of religion in that its Founders left instructions for an administrative framework, which they said would one day become the model of governance for a global community. In brief, it provides for yearly elections of Local Spiritual Assemblies and National Spiritual Assemblies.

The elections are conducted by secret ballot with no candidates or campaigning. Every member of the Bahá'í Community is expected to thoughtfully and prayerfully list the names of nine adult Bahá'ís, known to them, whom they believe to be mature, sincere, and responsible enough to be trusted with the governance of the Community. Every five years, the members of all the National Spiritual Assemblies gather at the World Centre to elect the Universal House of Justice in the same manner. It should be noted that decision-making power for the community is vested only in these bodies, not in the individuals who compose them. These bodies, in turn, function within the framework of laws set out by the Founders, which act as a kind of constitution.

The Bahá'í Administrative Order has two branches. One is the elected branch, described above. The other is the appointed branch (or Institution of the "learned"), which includes the Hands of the Cause, the Continental Boards of Counsellors, and the Auxiliary Boards and their assistants. Their role is advisory and inspirational, and they function as individuals, rather than as a body.

11. TWO WINGS OF A BIRD

> *Religion and science are the <u>two wings</u> upon which man's intelligence can soar into the heights, with which the human soul can progress. It is not possible to fly with one wing alone! Should a man try to fly with the wing of religion alone he would quickly fall into the quagmire of superstition, whilst on the other hand, with the wing of science alone he would also make no progress, but fall into the despairing slough of materialism.*
> [underlining added]

— 'Abdu'l-Bahá, *Paris Talks*, no. 44.14.

> *There must be an equality of rights between men and women. Women shall receive an equal privilege of education. This will enable them to qualify and progress in all degrees of occupation and accomplishment. For the world of humanity possesses <u>two wings</u>: man and woman. If one wing remains incapable and defective, it will restrict the power of the other, and full flight will be impossible. Therefore, the completeness and perfection of the human world are dependent upon the equal development of these two wings.*
> [underlining added]

— 'Abdu'l-Bahá, *The Promulgation of Universal Peace*, p. 318.

12. BAHÁ'Í TEACHINGS: THE ADAMIC CYCLE

Adamic Cycle. The period of time, approximately six thousand years, beginning with the revelation of Adam and ending with the Declaration of the Báb. Also called the "Prophetic era", the Adamic Cycle included a series of successive divine revelations which gave rise to the religions of Hinduism, Buddhism, Zoroastrianism, Judaism, Christianity, and Islam. The Declaration of the Báb in 1844 marked the end of the Adamic Cycle and the beginning of the 'Bahá'í Cycle,' or 'Era of Fulfillment.'

— Momen, *A Basic Bahá'í Dictionary*, p. 186.

BAHÁ'Í TEACHINGS: PROGRESSIVE REVELATION

Progressive Revelation. The concept that Divine Revelation is not final, but continuing. The concept of progressive revelation is founded on the belief that all the Greater Prophets of the past were Manifestations of God who appeared in different ages with teachings appropriate to the needs of the time: *in every Dispensation,* writes Bahá'u'lláh, *the light of Divine Revelation hath been vouchsafed unto men in direct proportion to their spiritual capacity.*

— Momen, *A Basic Bahá'í Dictionary*, p. 186.

BAHÁ'U'LLÁH'S TEACHINGS: THE MANIFESTATIONS OF GOD

In every age and cycle He hath, through the splendorous light shed by the Manifestations of His wondrous Essence, recreated all things, so that whatsoever reflecteth in the heavens and on the earth the signs of His glory may not be deprived of the outpourings of His mercy, nor despair of the showers of His favors. How all-encompassing are the wonders of His boundless grace! Behold how they have pervaded the whole of creation. Such is their virtue that not a single atom in the entire universe can be found which doth not declare the evidences of His might, which doth not glorify His holy Name, or is not expressive of the effulgent light of His unity. So perfect and comprehensive is His creation that no mind nor heart, however keen or pure, can ever grasp the nature of the most insignificant of His creatures; much less fathom the mystery of Him Who is the Day Star of Truth, Who is the invisible and unknowable Essence (p. 62).

How can I claim to have known Thee, when the entire creation is bewildered by Thy mystery, and how can I confess not to have known Thee when, lo, the whole universe proclaimeth Thy Presence and testifieth to Thy truth? The portals of Thy grace have throughout eternity been open, and the means of access unto Thy Presence made available, unto all created things, and the revelations of Thy matchless Beauty have at all times been imprinted upon the realities of all beings, visible and invisible. Yet, notwithstanding this most gracious favor, this perfect and consummate bestowal, I am moved to testify that Thy court of holiness and glory is immeasurably exalted above the knowledge of all else besides Thee, and the mystery of Thy Presence is inscrutable to every mind except Thine own. No one except Thyself can unravel the secret of Thy nature, and naught else but Thy transcendental Essence can grasp the reality of Thy unsearchable being (pp. 63-64).

Having created the world and all that liveth and moveth therein, He, through the direct operation of His unconstrained and sovereign Will, chose to confer upon man the unique distinction and capacity to know Him and to love Him — a capacity that must needs be regarded as the generating impulse and the primary purpose underlying the whole of creation (p. 65).

And since there can be no tie of direct intercourse to bind the one true God with His creation, and no resemblance whatever can exist between the transient and the Eternal, the contingent and the Absolute, <u>He hath ordained that in every age and dispensation a pure and stainless Soul be made manifest in the kingdoms of earth and heaven. Unto this subtle, this mysterious and ethereal Being he hath assigned a twofold nature; the physical, pertaining to the world of matter, and the spiritual, which is born of the substance of God Himself.</u> He hath, moreover, conferred upon Him a double station. <u>The first station</u>, which is related to His innermost reality, representeth Him as One Whose voice is the voice of God Himself. … <u>The second station</u> is the human station, exemplified by the following verses: "I am but a man like you" (pp. 66-67).
[underlining added]

From the foregoing passages and allusions it hath been made indubitably clear that in the kingdoms of earth and heaven there must needs be manifested a Being, an Essence Who shall act as a Manifestation and Vehicle for the transmission of the grace of the Divinity Itself, the Sovereign Lord of all (pp. 67-68).

Can one of sane mind ever seriously imagine that, in view of certain words the meaning of which he cannot comprehend, the portal of God's infinite guidance can ever be closed in the face of men? Can he ever conceive for these Divine Luminaries, these resplendent Lights either a beginning or an end? What outpouring flood can compare with the stream of His all-embracing grace, and what blessing can excel the evidences of so great and pervasive a mercy? There can be no doubt whatever that if for one moment the tide of His mercy and grace were to be withheld from this world, it would completely perish. For this reason, from the beginning that hath no beginning the portals of Divine mercy have been flung open to the face of all created things, and the clouds of Truth will continue to the end that hath no end to rain on the soil of human capacity, reality and personality their favors and bounties. Such hath been God's method continued from everlasting to everlasting (pp. 68–69).

— Bahá'u'lláh, *Gleanings*, Sections XXVI, XXVII,
  pp. 62–69.

13. IN THE GLORY OF THE FATHER

He Who in such dramatic circumstances was made to sustain the overpowering weight of so glorious a Mission was none other than the One Whom posterity will acclaim, and Whom innumerable followers already recognize as the Judge, the Lawgiver and Redeemer of all mankind, as the Organizer of the entire planet, as the Unifier of the children of men, as the Inaugurator of the long-awaited millennium, as the Originator of a new "Universal Cycle," as the Establisher of the Most Great Peace, as the Fountain of the Most Great Justice, as the Proclaimer of the coming of age of the entire human race, as the Creator of a new World Order, and as the Inspirer and Founder of a world civilization.

To Israel He was neither more nor less than the incarnation of the "Everlasting Father," the "Lord of Hosts" come down "with ten thousands of saints"; to Christendom Christ returned "in the glory of the Father;" to Shí'ah Islám the return of the Imám Husayn; to Sunní Islám the descent of the "Spirit of God" (Jesus Christ); to

the Zoroastrians the promised <u>Sh</u>áh-Bahrám; to the
Hindus the reincarnation of Krishna; to the Buddhists
the fifth Buddha.

— Shoghi Effendi, *God Passes By,* pp. 93–94.

14. LIFTING OF DISTINCTIONS: EMERGENCE OF THE FEMININE PRINCIPLE

Praised be God, the Pen of the Most High hath lifted distinctions from between His servants and handmaidens and, through His consummate favours and all-encompassing mercy, hath conferred upon all a station and rank on the same plane. He hath broken the back of vain imaginings with the sword of utterance and hath obliterated the perils of idle fancies through the pervasive power of His might.

— Bahá'u'lláh, qtd. in *Women,* p. 2.

The world in the past has been ruled by force, and man has dominated over woman by reason of his more forceful and aggressive qualities of body and mind. But the balance is already shifting — force is losing its weight and mental alertness, intuition, and the spiritual qualities of love and service, in which woman is strong, are gaining ascendancy. Hence the new age will be an age less masculine, and more permeated with the feminine ideals — or, to speak more exactly, will be an age in which the masculine and feminine elements of civilization will be more evenly balanced.

— 'Abdu'l-Bahá, qtd. in *Star of the West,* p. 4.

Pronunciation Guide

To Persian Names
for English-Speaking Readers

Column One, below, contains a list of letters used in Persian words that have been transliterated into the Roman alphabet. Shoghi Effendi has provided a full chart of the Persian and Roman letters in his Appendix to *The Dawn-Breakers* (p. 673).

Column Two lists the equivalent English sound, illustrated with English words.

Column Three lists important Bahá'í names containing these letters and sounds.

PERSIAN VOWEL	ENGLISH SOUND	BAHÁ'Í NAMES
a	account, random, focus	Bahá'í
á	arm, ah, on	Báb, Bahá'u'lláh
i	egg, best red	Ṭáhirih
í	eat, meet	Bahíyyih
u	off, awl, fall	Abdu'l-Bahá
ú	moon, soon	Rúḥíyyih

Khánum [**Kh** is a gutteral sound like the sound represented by "ch" in the German word *nacht*.]

'Abdu'l-Bahá [the character (') represents a pause. It is like the initial sound in "every.

References

'Abdu'l-Bahá. *Paris Talks: Addresses Given by 'Abdu'l-Bahá in 1911.* 12th ed. London: Bahá'í Publishing Trust, 1995.

'Abdu'l-Bahá. *The Promulgation of Universal Peace: Talks Delivered by 'Abdu'l-Bahá during His Visit to the United States and Canada in 1912.* Wilmette, IL: Bahá'í Publishing Trust, 1982.

'Abdu'l-Bahá. Report of remarks made aboard the *S.S. Cedric* on arrival in New York. Qtd. in *Star of the West.* Vol. 3, no.3.

'Abdu'l-Bahá. *Selections from the Writings of 'Abdu'l-Bahá.* Haifa: Bahá'í World Centre, 1978.

'Abdu'l-Bahá. *Tablets of the Divine Plan.* Wilmette, IL: Bahá'í Publishing Trust, 1993.

Bahá'u'lláh. *Gleanings from the Writings of Bahá'u'lláh.* Wilmette, IL: Bahá'í Publishing Trust, 1983.

Bahá'u'lláh. *The Hidden Words.* London: National Spiritual Assembly of the British Isles, 1949.

Bahá'u'lláh. "Násiri'd-Dín Sháh / Lawh-i-Sultan" in "Súrih of the Temple /Súriy-i-Haykal" in *The Summons of the Lord of Hosts: Tablets of Bahá'u'lláh.* Haifa: Bahá'í World Centre, 2002.

Bahá'u'lláh. "Law-i-Hikmat" in *Tablets of Bahá'u'lláh Revealed after the Kitab-i-Aqdas.* Willmette, IL: Bahá'í Publishing Trust, 1988.

Bahíyyih Khánum: The Greatest Holy Leaf. A compilation from Bahá'í sacred texts and writings of the Guardian of the Faith and Bahíyyih Khánum's own letters. Research Department at the Bahá'í World Centre. Haifa: World Centre Publications, 1982.

Cheyne, T.K. *The Reconciliation of Races and Religions.* Adams and Charles Black, 1914.

Cooper, John W. *Our Father in Heaven: Christian Faith and Inclusive Language for God.* Grand Rapids, MI: Baker Books, 1998.

Garis, M.R. *Martha Root: Lioness at the Threshold.* Wilmette, IL: Bahá'í Publishing Trust, 1983.

Holley, Horace. "Survey of Current Bahá'í Activities, 1928–1930: An International Bahá'í Teacher." In *The Bahá'í World* [Formerly: *Bahá'í Year Book*]: *A Biennial International Record, 1928–1930.* Vol. 3. Compiled by National Spiritual Assembly of the Bahá'ís of the United States and Canada. New York: Bahá'í Publishing Committee, 1930, p. 46.

Lenz, Elinor, and Barbara Myerhoff. *The Feminization of America: How Women's Values Are Changing Our Public and Private Lives.* Los Angeles: Jeremy P. Tarcher, Inc., 1985.

Lights of Guidance. Compiled by Helen Hornby. New Delhi: Bahá'í Publishing Trust, 1983.

Momen, Wendi, ed. *A Basic Bahá'í Dictionary.* Oxford: George Ronald, 1991.

Nabíl-i-A'zam. *The Dawn-Breakers: Nabíl's Narrative of the Early Days of the Bahá'í Revelation,* edited and translated by Shoghi Effendi. Wilmette, IL: Bahá'í Publishing Trust, 1970.

Pantel, Pauline Schmitt, ed. *A History of Women in the West: From Ancient Goddesses to Christian Saints.* Vol. 1. General Editors Georges Duby and Michelle Perrot. Cambridge, MA, and London, England: The Belknap Press of Harvard University Press, 1994.

Rabbání, Rúḥíyyih. *The Priceless Pearl.* England: Broadwater Press, 1969.

Root, Martha L. "A Bahá'í Pilgrimage to South America," TS, personal papers of Emanuel Reimer. Portions of this account were published in *Star of the West*, 11 (13 July 1920), pp. 107-11, 113-18.

Shoghi Effendi. *The Advent of Divine Justice.* Wilmette, IL: Bahá'í Publishing Trust, 1963.

Shoghi Effendi. *God Passes By.* Wilmette, IL: Bahá'í Publishing Trust, 1974.

Shoghi Effendi. *The Promised Day Is Come.* Wilmette, IL: Bahá'í Publishing Trust, 1996.

Shoghi Effendi to Root, December 1929. Martha L. Root Papers, National Bahá'í Archives, Wilmette, IL [According to the editor of *Martha Root: Lioness at the Threshold,* an approved translation of this letter does not yet exist; consequently, this translation cannot be considered authentic.]

Women: Extracts from the Writings of Bahá'u'lláh, 'Abdu'l-Bahá, Shoghi Effendi, and the Universal House of Justice, comp. Research Department of the Universal House of Justice. Thornhill, ON: Bahá'í Canada Publications, 1986.

Women: A Compilation of Extracts from the Bahá'í Writings, Rev. ed., London: Bahá'í Publishing Trust, 1990.

For more information about the Bahá'í Faith go to:
www.bahai.org